Encouraging Your Wife

A Practical Guide to Encourage Your Bride

ILYNMW Publishing
Atlanta Georgia

Dedication

This book is dedicated to my Bride and the love of my life - Debbie.

TFSY

ILYNMW

YAMBFES

Other Books by Paul Beersdorf

- Flowers on Tuesday

- 52 Things I Wish My Father Had Taught Me About Marriage & Family

- The 100 Most Important Words

Contents

Acknowledgements

I want to thank all of our family and friends who helped contribute content to this book. My Bride is especially good at encouraging me and she has a real knack for knowing just what to say and when to say it. I love her so very much and appreciate the friendship, love and support that she gives me.

Introduction

What is encouragement? Here is a clinical definition:

Definition - Encouragement - something that makes someone more determined, hopeful, or confident

What are some other words for encouragement?

Reassurance
Inspiration
Praise
Reinforcement
Boost
Support

These are all great words!   All of these words should be evident in our lives as we strive to encourage our Bride.

The goal of this book is to create men who will become encouraging "machines" For some men; this is already second nature.   They encourage their Bride on a regular basis and build her up as a wife, mother, daughter and friend

However, there are many men who could use a 'nudge" and learn how to better encourage their bride. This book will provide you some creative and practical resources and guides to help you encourage your bride. You must become a student of your Bride and never stop studying her and learning about her and her needs, wants and desires.

Below are some great verses that describe how blessed we are to have the Brides we have. God knew that we needed someone to walk through this life with and he graciously provided us an incredible companion.

Genesis 2:18
The LORD God said, "It is not good for the man to be alone. I will make a helper suitable for him."

Ephesians 5:25
Husbands, love your wives, just as Christ also loved the church and gave Himself up for her,

Proverbs 18: 22
He who finds a wife finds a good thing And obtains favor from the LORD.

Proverbs 31:10
An excellent wife, who can find? For her worth is far above jewels.

Proverbs 19:14
House and wealth are an inheritance from fathers, but a prudent wife is from the LORD.

Mark 10:9
What therefore God has joined together let no man separate."

Bring Your "A" Game

What does it mean to bring your "A" game? It means that you Bride does not get the "left overs" of your time, talents and treasures. It means that she is not the second or third thought you have for the day, but the first thought you have for the day.

Remember when you were first dating? You could not wait to spend time with her. You anticipated going out on the date and the activities you would enjoy.

You would buy her flowers; you would show up unexpectedly and take her out to lunch. She was constantly on your heart and mind. You cleaned up, you dressed up, you showed up on time! You opened her door and held her hand. When she walked into room you smiled and your heart leapt.

In other words, you were prepared, thoughtful, considerate and kind. You brought your "A" game when you were pursuing her and she was the target of your affections.

She needs, wants and desires for you to bring your "A" game every day. She wants you to want her! Whether you are a newlywed or have been married for over 20 years, it is your responsibility to continue to pursue your Bride and make her feel different, better and special.

You can do this through continuous encouragement and thoughtfulness. It will take some work and investment, but mostly you just need to be intentional about making her a priority in your life.

By the way - she is so worth it!!

Communicating With Your Bride

Encouraging your Bride is all about making a positive investment in her.   One of the primary means of encouraging your Bride will be how you communicate with her on a daily basis. Note that I said "daily basis".   You should be communicating with your Bride each and every day!

What do I mean by communication?

- Verbal - what you say
- Non-verbal - your actions and gestures/facial expressions
- Text
- E-mail
- Snail mail
- Notes
- Social Media posts (Facebook, Twitter, etc.)
- Video conference
- Smoke Signals
- Telegram
- Semaphore flags

Positive communication is one of the keys to a great relationship and a key building block for a long term future together.   In the following chapters, you will read;

- Things she needs to see you do when you are communicating with her

- Things she needs to hear you say

- Things she needs to read (from you)

It is your job to become a "communications expert" in regards to your Bride. She deserves your very best effort each and every day. It will not be easy, but it is a task worthy of a real man.

Yes, real men say "I love you" and mean it!

Communication Skills
Things she needs to see you doing when you communicate with her.

When you are communicating with your Bride your actions can be just as important as the words you are using. Here are some suggested actions to consider when communicating with your Bride.

- Put away your cell phone and focus on her

- Look at her when you are talking and smile

- Turn off the TV (do not just put it on mute)

- Listen without solving (this is tough, but train yourself to just listen). What I have done is actually ask my Bride if she is looking for a solution of if she just wants me to listen. Ask specific questions!

- Do not look at your watch, fidget, or act disinterested in her story (pay attention)

- Tell her about your day and include as many details as possible

- Praise her in public

- Praise her even when she is not around (yes I know she cannot see you doing this, but it is an intentional action on your part and a conscience effort to always be positive about your Bride)

- Take her side in arguments with kids, family and friends

- If you are running early or late let her know

- Pay attention to the way she looks

- If you cannot sympathize then empathize.

- Be that shoulder she can lean on

- Make her a priority! She will know this by the amount of time and energy you focus on her.

- When in doubt, ask your Bride how you can do a better job communicating with her.

It is just not good enough for you to say that you are not good at communicating. Communication is a skill that can be learned, honed and perfected by anyone who is willing to put in the time, energy and effort to be a better communicator.

The Things She Needs to Hear You Say

Your Bride needs to hear you offer encouraging words all the time. According to Harvard Business Review, the highest performing teams in business offer positive comments almost six times more than they offer negative comments.

Interestingly enough, Dr. John Gottman has studied married couples and he suggests that the best ratio of positive to negative comments is 5 to 1.

No matter the source, the idea is that we should be praising and encouraging our Brides much more than we are offering criticism.

Below are over 100 suggested things you can say to your Bride if you want to encourage her. These are not in any particular order; this is a list that my Bride and I compiled, along with the help from some of our friends and family.

Commit today to using these phrases on a frequent basis with your Bride.

Below are the different sections that will be covered in this chapter:

- Encouragement When She is Hurting
- Encouraging her Physical Attributes
- Encouragement For Her as a Mother
- Encouragement for Her as Your Bride
- Spiritual Encouragement for Her
- General Encouragement For Her
- Encouragement by Time Together
- Encouragement When she is Tired
- Encouragement For The Long Run
- Encouragement For Her Decisions
- Encouragement for her Home
- Other Encouragement

Remember that you can never tell you Bride these two things too much:

1. *"I love you"*

2. *"You are beautiful"*

Encouragement When She is Hurting

- *"I love you no matter what"*

- *"I am here for you"*

- *"How can I serve you better?"*

- *"I love you no matter what!"*

- *"I believe in you"*

- *"It going to be OK"*

- *"When push comes to shove, I will always choose you"*

- *"We can get through this together, you are not alone"*

- *"This too shall pass"*

- *"I know you are going through a rough time, when you are ready to talk; I will be here for you"*

- *"I fully support you"*

- *"Don't give up and don't give in - stand your ground and I support you 100%"*

- *"Would you like to talk?"*

- *"Tomorrow is a new day"*

Encouragement When She is Hurting

- *"I don't completely understand what you are feeling, but I love you no matter what"*

- *"Try to forget todays troubles, and focus on the blessings"*

- *"You are not a failure"*

- *"Do you need a hug?"*

- *"You are important to me"*

- *"God is in control"*

- *"I love you no matter what"*

Encouraging her Physical Attributes

- *"I love you no matter what"*

- *"You are beautiful"*

- *"I love you no matter what"*

- *"You look great"*

- *"Will you wear that _____ that you look so good in?*

- *"I really like that outfit."*

- *"You smell good"*

- *"I love looking into your eyes"*

- *"I love watching you from across the room"*

- *"I love your laugh"*

- *"I love being seen in public with you on my arm"*

- *"When I think about you, it brings a smile to my face"*

- Comment positively on what she is wearing

- Try to notice the little things like the shoes, earrings, necklace (the accessories) and tell her how nice they look on her.

Encouraging her Physical Attributes

- *"I love falling asleep in your arms"*

- *"You are elegant"*

- *"You have an incredible smile"*

- *"I love the way you fixed your hair"*

- *"Your new hair cut looks fantastic"*

- *"Wow! You look fantastic in that outfit"*

- *"You have beautiful eyes"*

- *"You are the most beautiful woman I have ever seen"*

- *"No one compares to you"*

- *"I love waking up with you each morning"*

- *"You are beautiful"*

- Feel free to positively comment on other parts of her body. You should know your Bride well enough to know what part to comment on and which parts to leave alone. Be wise!

Encouragement for Her as a Mother

- "You are a great mother"

- "You are doing a great job with the kids"

- "I love how you pour your life into our children"

- "Thank you for being such a positive influence for our family"

- "I want our girls to grow up just like you"

- Thank you for being such a great example for our children"

- "What would we do without you?"

- "You bring honor to our family"

- "I would not want anyone else to be the mother of our children"

- "Thanks for being such a hard worker"

- "Thank you for making our family a priority"

- "Our children are a reflection of you"

- "You are a blessing to me and the kids"

- "You are a great example to other young mothers"

- "You make beautiful babies"

Encouragement for Her as a Mother

- *"Thank you for setting the example for our boys future wives"*

- *"You are an incredibly hard worker - thank you"*

- *"I love watching you play with the kids"*

- *"Words cannot express how much I appreciate what you do for our family"*

- *"You are a beautiful mother"*

- *"You are the most beautiful pregnant woman"*

- *"I love you no matter what""*

Encouragement for Her as Your Bride

- *"You are my beautiful Bride"*

- *"Thanks for saying yes"* (this is a reference to her saying yes to marrying you)

- *"I love you"*

- *"You are my best friend"*

- *"I need you"*

- *"I want you"*

- *"Thank you for _____ "(you fill in the blank)*

- *"You are a great wife (Bride)"*

- *"You make me a better man"*

- *"You are so beautiful"*

- *"You complete me"*

- *"I am a lucky dog!"*

- *"You are a blessing to me"*

- *"You make me want to be a better man"*

- *"I am the luckiest man in the world"*

Spiritual Encouragement for Her

- *"How can I pray for you?"*

- *"Let's pray together"*

- *"I praise God for you "*

- *"I've been praying for you"*

- *"When I pray to God, I thank Him for you"*

- *"You are a Proverbs 31 woman"*

- *"I praise God for bringing you into my life"*

- *'I love that the fruits of the spirit are evident in your life."*

- *"You are such a blessing to me"*

- *"I love how you use your skills and abilities to bless others"*

- *"Thank you for serving others"*

- *"It is so obvious that you love God"*

- *"Let's worship together as a family"*

- *"I have a new devotion book I would us to use together"*

- *"I love you no matter what"*

General Encouragement for Her

- *"I love you"*

- *"You are so beautiful"*

- *"Great job!"*

- *"I am proud of you"*

- *"I trust you"*

- *"You are incredibly talented"*

- *"You can do it!"*

- *"I have confidence in you"*

- *"I love your positive **can do** attitude"*

- *"Have I told you lately how much I love you?"*

- *"No one compares to you"*

- *"You are an incredible woman"*

- *"You can do anything you set your mind to"*

- *"You got this, girl"*

- *"I love you"*

- *"You are beautiful"*

Encouragement by Time Together

- *"Would you like to go on a date?"*

- *"What would you like to do today?"*

- *"I have a surprise for you"*

- *"Here are some tickets for* _____"

- *"Let's get away for the weekend"*

- *"I cannot wait to see you!"*

- *"Let's snuggle"*

- *"You choose"* (dinner date, TV stations, music etc)

- *"Would you like to dance?"*

- *"You take the remote and pick something for us to watch"*

- *"I have hired a babysitter and we are going out this weekend"*

- *"Let's celebrate"*

- *"Let's go for a walk"*

- *"I have a song I want to sing to you"*

- *"I wrote a poem for you"*

Encouragement by Time Together

- *"Let's grab a cup of coffee and talk"*

- *"I just love spending time with you"*

- *"Spending time with you is such a blessing"*

- *"Grab a blanket and let's go look at the stars and make a wish"*

Encouragement When she is Tired

- *"I love you no matter what"*

- *"I know you have had a tough day, let's get some takeout for dinner tonight."*

- *"Sit back and relax, I got this"*

- *"Let me watch the kids tonight and you enjoy some time to yourself"*

- *"Make me a "honey do" list and I will get it done"*

- *"How can I help you?"*

- *"I will help the kids with their homework tonight"*

- *"Let me put the kids to bed tonight"*

- *"I fixed dinner and I will clean the kitchen afterwards"*

- *"I filled the tub with hot water - enjoy"*

- *"I got you some chocolate"*

- *"I'll take care of the laundry and kitchen"*

- *"Would you like a massage?"*

Encouragement for The Long Run

- *"I only want to walk through life with you by my side"*

- *"I want to grow old with you"*

- *"You are the only one for me"*

- *"I will never leave you nor forsake you"*

- *"Nothing can separate us"*

- *"We are ONE!"*

- *"I choose you"*

- *"We make a great team"*

- *"You are the only one for me"*

- *"You make life worth living"*

- *"I could not do this without you"*

- *"Thanks for being there for me"*

- *"When I am with you, all my troubles are far away"*

- *"When the going gets tough, I will be there right by your side"*

- *"If I had to do it all over again, I would choose you"*

Encouragement for Her Decisions

- *"I love you no matter what"*

- *"I love how you handled that situation"*

- *"You were right"*

- *"I trust you with our finances"*

- *"I appreciate that you always have our best interests in mind"*

- *"That must have been really hard for you do say - thank you for having the courage to speak up"*

- *"Thank you for making wise decisions"*

- *"I know we can always trust you"*

- *"Thank you for sweating the small details"*

- *"What do you think about _____"*

- *"I could use some advice"*

- *"Thank you for your honesty"*

<u>Encouragement for Her Home</u>

- *"You make our home a sanctuary of peace and tranquility*

- *"You make everything more beautiful"*

- *"I love how you make our house a home"*

- *"That meal you cooked was fantastic"*

- *"Thank you for planning out the meals each week"*

- *"You are an incredible cook"*

- *"Your garden is so beautiful, you have a real green thumb"*

- *"I cannot wait to come home each day"*

- *"Our home is so beautiful, thank you"*

- *"I really appreciate how you have decorated our home"*

- *"Thank you for opening our home to bless others"*

- *"Thank you for "magic drawers"* - This is a reference to always having clean laundry in your drawers

- *"It obvious that you have poured yourself into our home"*

- *"Thank you for taking care of the cooking and cleaning - you are such a blessing to me and our family"*

Other Encouragement

- *"I missed you, I am glad you a finally home"*

- *"When we are not together, I don't feel the same"*

- *"I love how disciplined you are"*

- *"You have been a great sibling to your brothers and sisters"*

- *"I am sorry for _____"*

- *"Will you forgive me for _____"*

- *"I forgive you"*

- *"You are very talented with _____"*

- *"I want you to pursue your dreams!"*

- *"How can I be a dream maker for you?"*

- *"I took care of that _____ that I know you do not like to do"*

- *"You are a great daughter to your parents"*

- *"I am very proud of the way you serve your parents"*

- *"I love how you continue to make your parents a priority in your life"*

As with all the lists and suggestions in book, the things you need to say to your Bride is not comprehensive. It is meant to be a thought starter and reminder of how you need to communicate with your Bride.

I would encourage you to use this list and see how many of these sayings you can use over the course of a year. It goes without saying that you should be sincere and that this should not feel forced or contrived. You may be uncomfortable with some of these things, but she will appreciate your effort.

Remember - she is worth it!

Notes Page

Use the page to take notes and suggested actions or next steps.

Things She Needs to Read

In addition to the verbal communication you will have with your Bride, you can also take the opportunity to work on your writing skills and creativity to encourage your Bride.

Below are some suggestions.   I would encourage you to use all of the technology at your disposal to encourage your Bride (cell phone, computer, tablet, apps, pen and paper etc.)

- A quick text in the morning after you get to work to say "hello - I love you"

- Text her throughout the day to tell her how beautiful she is and how much you miss her.

- Write her a "real" love letter or card and put in in the mail.   Take the time to buy a bunch of stamps.

- Invest in some nice personal stationary when you write her those notes.

Things She Needs to Read

- Compose a poem or song dedicated to her (there are actually websites that can help you do this).

- Send her a text while you are out running errands and just tell her you are thinking about her

- Send her an e-mail with a greeting card attached

- Cover her car with post it notes that say "I love you"

- Leave little notes for her in following places :

  o On her pillow

  o In her car

  o In different draws around your house

  o In the refrigerator

- Use your social media to complement and praise your Bride. Your Facebook, Twitter, Instagram etc. should resonate with your love and admiration for your Bride. There should be no question as to who your best friend is.

Things She Needs to Read

- Send her a text or email everyday with a new way to say how much you love and appreciate her.

- Hire a sky writing service and have them write here a note in the sky.

- Rent a bill board and surprise her with a message.

- Go to a sporting event and have then put up a message to her during the game.

You know your Bride better than anyone, so take all of these ideas as suggestions and use the ones that you know will resonate with her.

Notes Page

Use the page to take notes and suggested actions or next steps.

Little Things
You Need to Do

- A minimum of three kisses each day (in morning when you leave for work, when you get home, when you say good night). Remember this is just the minimum

- Open doors for your bride

- Hold her hand - at home, at church, on a date, on a walk etc.

- Put the lid down on the toilet

- Wash her car

- Put the kids to bed (better yet, draw her a bath and then put the kids to bed)

- Run some of the errands for her

- Do the grocery shopping

Little Things You Need to Do

- Clean up your messes (both in the house and in the garage, basement or yard)

- Wash up (our Brides do not typically like dirty and stinky)

- Pick up after yourself (she is not your mother, she is your Bride)

- If you handle the money - take some time periodically to bring her up to speed on the finances

- Be responsible with your money and have a clear family budget

- Don't get carried away with hobbies (be considerate about how much time and money you invest in your hobbies)

- Play with your children

- Pray together

- Pray with the whole family

Little Things You Need to Do

- Worship together

- Buy her Chocolate

- Serve others together

- Cook her a meal (breakfast, lunch or dinner) and then clean up the mess

- Turn the coffee on in the morning (even if you do not drink coffee)

- If you have little children, help with bed time routines (bathing, brushing teeth, story time, getting dressed etc)

- Rub her - neck, feet, shoulders (whatever she enjoys)

- Get up in the morning with the little ones and let her grab some extra sleep

- Take your daughters out on dates

- Teach your sons to love and respect their mother - be a positive role model for him

Little Things You Need to Do

- Pillow talk!

- Dress nicely for your Bride (she really does not like the "wife beater" shirt - she was just being polite when she said she liked it).

- Take care of yourself (exercise and stay fit - do not let your body go downhill)

- Breakfast in bed (and not just on mother's day)

- If you travel and are on the road a lot, invest in the technology so you can video conference with your Bride through Skype or other application.

- Hugs are always a good physical reminder to your Bride how much you love her. If you are not a "hugger", I would encourage you to become one! A hug is just a physical way of saying "I love you".

Little Things You Need to Do

- Keep her car well maintained and if you travel or have a very busy schedule, purchase AAA or other auto club service, so she can have peace of mind while driving her car around.

Notes Page

Use the page to take notes and suggested actions or next steps.

Investing in Your Bride

All of these suggestions will require an investment of your time and some of them will require an investment of your money. I can almost guarantee that you will see a great "return on investment" by focusing on your Bride.

My only caveat is that these investments should be from the heart and not driven by an act of contrition on your part.

First let's start with things you cannot forget:

- Do not forget your anniversary

- Do not forget her birthday

- Do no forget the kids birthdays

- Do not forget Valentine's Day

- Do not forget Mother's day

- Do not forget other important events (games, shows, parties, gatherings, etc.)

Investing in Your Bride

Also, here are some things you typically **should NOT** buy for your Bride (yes I recognize there will be some exceptions to these rules). Know your Bride and what she likes and dislikes.

- Power Tools (or any tool for that matter)

- Household appliances (e.g. Toaster, Blender, Vacuum)

- Seasons tickets to **your** favorite sporting event

- Utensils

- Lawnmower or yard tools

- TV, Computer or Electronic Gaming

- Towels or Sheets

- Dishes

- Hunting Gear

Now how can you invest in your Bride?

- Chocolate! (although my Bride loves Cake so you need to know what your Bride loves and give her that)

Investing in Your Bride

- Buy her flowers on a Tuesday! (just because you love her)

- Get her a gift certificate for a manicure and or pedicure

- Hire a cleaning service to come in and do spring cleaning

- Hire a lawn service to beautify the yard

- Give here the day off to enjoy some time for herself

- Diamonds are a girl's best friend - although you need to understand if this will appeal to your Bride or not. My Bride does not really care for jewelry, but loves things that will decorate the house.

- Buy her a romantic song to download to her phone, computer or tablet

- Name a star after her

- Learn a new recipe and cook her a complete meal

Investing in Your Bride

- Hire a babysitter on a regular basis so you can have time alone.

- Take her shopping for a new outfit

- Make her a CD with all of her favorite songs

- Pick some wildflowers for her - my Bride loves this!

- Treat her to a day at the spa

- Make vacations a priority (you should consider this an investment and not a cost)

- Gift certificates to her favorite stores

- Upgrade her cell phone

- Buy her a thoughtful gift for the house/apartment

- Hire a singing telegram

- Make out a calendar of events for the year and surprise her with all the time you are going to invest in her

- Make her a coupon book filled with different date ideas that she can redeem at any time

Investing in Your Bride

- If she travels for work- make the effort to go to the airport and meet her for a quick date (having some flowers with you is probably a good idea as well)

- Fill the house with love notes - leave them everywhere

- Hire a musician to come to your house and serenade your Bride

- Enroll here in a "Coffee Club" that will send her a new type of coffee once per month (you can also do this with Candy, Flowers and many other products)

- If she loves shoes (and who doesn't) - get her a gift certificate to Zappos.com. A great site that allows you to try shoes and if they don't fit, easily return them.

- Subscription to her favorite magazine

- Plants for the house or yard (trees and flowers are usually a good choice)

Investing in Your Bride

- Put some money in an envelope and label it "mad money" and tell her to enjoy herself.

- Clean up the garage and or basement

- Take care of the yard

- Do the laundry

- Clean and vacuum the house (especially the kitchen)

- Take the kids for the day (or the weekend) and give her some time to herself

- Support her hobbies and talents by giving her the time to enjoy and pursue them.

- Buy some books on marriage and family enrichment and study them yourself! Apply what you learn from these books in your marriage.

- Attend a men's conference at your local church or out of town (she will appreciate that you are trying to become a better husband and father)

. _Investing in Your Bride_

- Create a "slush fund" to spend on her by putting money

  in a jar that you would normally spend on a cup of

  coffee. Do this for 30 days and you will have quite a bit

  of money to treat your Bride.

This list could be endless, but the key point is that you need to understand what will resonate best with your Bride and then make the investment in her. She will very much appreciate that thought and if you have made some wise choices, she will also appreciate the gift as well.

Notes Page

Use the page to take notes and suggested actions or next steps.

Spending Time
With Your Bride

(Dating your Bride - it does not have to be expensive)

There is no better way to encourage your Bride than spending time with her!

Below are a number of examples of ways to spend time with your Bride. Some of them will require an investment (note I did not say cost) but many of them will only require you to be thoughtful and invest your time.

- Go for a walk - Hold her hand on that walk!

- Go to a wedding together and repeat your vows along with the couple getting married

- Attend a local high school sports teams game (you don't even have to know anybody playing - pretend you are in high school again)

- Dance with your Bride - you can do this at home or on a date.

- Watch the sunrise

Spending Time with Your Bride

- Watch the sunset

- Go on picnic

- Dinner and a movie

- Go to a carnival

- Learn to play tennis together

- Make it a Netflix night

- Progressive fast food date (Salad at Wendy's, French Fries at McDonalds, sandwich at Burger King, milkshake at Dairy Queen)

- Listen to some of her favorite music together

- Take her to a concert

- Buy her seasons tickets to Broadway plays in your town (this way you have guaranteed date for 6-8 times each year)

- Make a "wish" list together and try to accomplish one of the wishes.

Spending Time with Your Bride

- Attend a marriage enrichment seminar

- Get away for a long weekend together

- Break out the beach chairs in the living room and watch a fun beach movie

- Take her out dancing

- Go to a "pick your own" farm and pick some fruit

- If you don't know how to dance, sign up for dance lessons together

- Sit and drink a cup of coffee together in the morning (or at night)

- Fix a meal of her favorite foods (and clean up the mess)

- Surprise her at work with a lunch date

- Go for a hike in a national or state park

- Go play Frisbee

- Go thrift store shopping and look to buy a gift for each other under $10

Spending Time with Your Bride

- Put a blanket out in the yard and look at the stars

- Find a new recipe and cook it together

- Go to a local museum

- Go to yard/garage sales on a Saturday morning

- Take a tour of a local company

- Start a garden

- Book a cruise

- Go to a trampoline park for the day

- Go buy a kite on a windy day and have some fun

- Bowling anyone?

- Join the local gym or YMCA and exercise together

- Go to the farmers market

- Visit antique stores

- Attend a local festival

- Go to the zoo

- Go shopping for a new car (even if you don't need one)

Spending Time with Your Bride

- Try French Fries from all the local fast food joints and vote on your favorite
- Work on a home project together
- Learn a new language together
- Go to a water park together
- Read her a book of poetry
- Go to a local park on a partly cloudy day and talk about the different shapes of the clouds
- Play hide and seek in the house
- Go to a stable and learn to ride horses
- Break out Monopoly (or other board game)
- Spend the evening watching hilarious YouTube videos
- Go swinging at the playground
- Pretend you are in middle school again and go skating
- During the holidays, go look at houses that are decorated

Spending Time with Your Bride

- Find a waterfall near you and drive or hike to it

- Go to the circus

- Rent a canoe

- Head to the local coffee shop and just chill

- Go white water rafting

- Wake up early and go to the local bakery or doughnut shop and get something fresh

- Find a "dollar" theater and watch movies all day

- Go to the mall food court (try a least one new thing)

- Get some ice cream at Dairy Queen

- Go to Trip Advisor and find some cool things to do around your home that you probably never heard of.

- Volunteer together at a food bank for the day

- Help build a home with Habitat for Humanity

- Go to a play at the local high school or college

Spending Time with Your Bride

- Go to YELP/Urban Spoon or other internet sight and find a new restaurant to try.

- Put a bunch of these date ideas in a bag and have her pick one.

- Pack a suitcase for her and pick her up at work for a surprise weekend away

- Watch some of her favorite TV shows with her (e.g. HGTV)

- Grab a blanket and snuggle on the couch

- If you have a fire place, have dinner in front of the fire

- Find a drive- in movie theater

- Dinner and a Redbox movie

- Go to a comedy club

- Jump in the car and take a drive (doesn't matter where)

- If you live in the city, jump on the Train and take a ride

- Rent a cabin in the woods for the weekend

Spending Time with Your Bride

- Wake up at 2am and head to a local 24 hour restaurant (Waffle House, Ihop, Denny's etc.)

- Give your Bride a massage along with chocolate covered strawberries (playing some romantic music and candle light is also a really good idea)

- Pop some popcorn, grab a pen and paper and make out your bucket list together

- Put together a puzzle

- Learn to play golf together

- Enroll in some community classes together

- Learn a new hobby you can both enjoy (like photography)

- Go rappelling

- Manicure and pedicure together

- Karaoke anyone?

- Study the Song of Solomon together

Spending Time with Your Bride

- Enjoy each season outdoors with different activities no matter how hot or cold

- Rake a huge pile of leaves and then jump into it

- Who said Disney was just for kids

- Rent a condo for the week and just enjoy each other's company (at the beach or in the mountains)

- Go backpacking or camping

- Go to your Alma Mater and stroll the campus

- Break out the video games and pizza and make a night of it.

- Go skeet shooting

- Nerf gun war (whoever wins cooks dinner)

- Visit the humane society and pet the animals

- Grab a line and go fishing

- Wander around Walmart

- Make s'mores over a fire (or in the microwave)

Spending Time with Your Bride

- Bake some cookies or a cake together

- Get massages together at the spa

- Go to an auction

- Have a "staycation" and do all the touristy stuff in your town

- Go watch fireworks

- Run through a field of wildflowers together

- Take a nap together

- Ask her what she would like to do and then go do it

This was obviously not a complete list of all the different things you can do to spend time with you Bride, but it would certainly keep you busy for quite a while. The main point is that you should be spending both quality and quantity time with your Bride. I encourage you to be creative and talk to your friends and neighbors about different date ideas and how to spend time with your Bride.

Finally - one of the things you will want to strive for is to have at least one date night per week. One weekend away two to three times each year, and a full week away every 2-3 years.

Notes Page

Use the page to take notes and suggested actions or next steps.

Encouraging Quotes

There is only one way to avoid criticism: do nothing, say nothing, and be nothing. *–Aristotle*

Believe you can and you're halfway there. *–Theodore Roosevelt*

Winning isn't everything, but wanting to win is. *–Vince Lombardi*

"Never consider the possibility of failure; as long as you persist, you will be successful." *- Brian Tracy*

Fall seven times, stand up eight. *~Japanese Proverb*

Few things can help an individual more than to place responsibility on him, and to let him know that you trust him. *–Booker T. Washington*

"One has to remember that every failure can be a stepping stone to something better." *Col. Harland Sanders*

"A diamond is merely a lump of coal that did well under pressure." *Unknown*

Encouraging Quotes

It is not the mountain we conquer but ourselves.
Edmund Hillary

The best time to plant a tree was 20 years ago. The second best time is now. **Chinese Proverb**

"Never give up on what you really want to do. The person with big dreams is more powerful than one with all the facts." - **Unknown**

If the wind will not serve, take to the oars. - **Latin Proverb**

*An unexamined life is not worth living. –***Socrates**

When you encourage others, you in the process are encouraged because you're making a commitment and difference in that person's life. Encouragement really does make a difference. **Zig Ziglar**

*You can't fall if you don't climb. But there's no joy in living your whole life on the ground. –***Unknown**

''Age is no barrier. It's a limitation you put on your mind.'' -
Jackie Joyner-Kersee

Do what you can, where you are, with what you have. –
Teddy Roosevelt

Encouraging Quotes

A word of encouragement from a teacher to a child can change a life. A word of encouragement from a spouse can save a marriage. A word of encouragement from a leader can inspire a person to reach her potential.   **John C. Maxwell**

Nothing is impossible, the word itself says, "I'm possible!" –**Audrey Hepburn**

Nine tenths of education is encouragement.
Anatole France

If you're going through hell, keep going. -**Winston Churchill**

Either write something worth reading or do something worth writing. –**Benjamin Franklin**

I ask not for a lighter burden, but for broader shoulders.
-**Jewish Proverb**

"Everything will be OK in the end, if it's not OK, it's not the end.''
- **Unknown**

If you are a leader, you should never forget that everyone needs encouragement. And everyone who receives it - young or old, successful or less-than-successful, unknown or famous - is changed by it. **John C. Maxwell**

Encouraging Quotes

"When you come to the end of your rope, tie a knot and hang on." - **Franklin D. Roosevelt**

Twenty years from now you will be more disappointed by the things that you didn't do than by the ones you did do, so throw off the bowlines, sail away from safe harbor, catch the trade winds in your sails. Explore, Dream, Discover. – **Mark Twain**

If you can dream it, you can achieve it. – **Zig Ziglar**

If you want to lift yourself up, lift up someone else. –**Booker T. Washington**

"Don't be discouraged. It's often the last key in the bunch that opens the lock." - **Unknown**

Two roads diverged in a wood, and I – I took the one less traveled by, And that has made all the difference. –**Robert Frost**

A person who never made a mistake never tried anything new. – **Albert Einstein**

"When one door closes another door opens; but we so often look so long and so regretfully upon the closed door, that we do not see the ones which open for us." - **Alexander Graham Bell**

Encouraging Quotes

"Instruction does much, but encouragement everything."
— *Johann Wolfgang von Goethe*

"Instead of giving myself reasons why I can't, I give myself reasons why I can." - **Author Unknown**

Education costs money. But then so does ignorance. –**Sir Claus Moser**

You miss 100% of the shots you don't take. –**Wayne Gretzky**

Whether you think you can or you think you can't, you're right. – **Henry Ford**

A bend in the road is not the end of the road... unless you fail to make the turn. - **Unknown**

Life is 10% what happens to me and 90% of how I react to it. – **Charles Swindoll**

Remember no one can make you feel inferior without your consent. – **Eleanor Roosevelt**

Encouraging Quotes

"I don't regret the things I've done, I regret the things I didn't do when I had the chance." – **Unknown**

You can never cross the ocean until you have the courage to lose sight of the shore. –**Christopher Columbus**

When it is dark enough, you can see the stars.
Ralph Waldo Emerson

"In order to succeed, your desire for success should be greater than your fear of failure." – **Bill Cosby**

The difficulties of life are intended to make us better, not bitter.
Unknown

"The pessimist sees difficulty in every opportunity. The optimist sees opportunity in every difficulty" - **Winston Churchill**

"I'd rather be a failure at something I love than a success at something I hate." - **George Burns**

I didn't fail the test. I just found 100 ways to do it wrong. –
Benjamin Franklin

Encouraging Quotes

People often say that motivation doesn't last. Well, neither does bathing. That's why we recommend it daily. –**Zig Ziglar**

It does not matter how slowly you go as long as you do not stop. – **Confucius**

"You may not realize it when it happens, but a kick in the teeth may be the best thing in the world for you." **Walt Disney**

It's not the years in your life that count. It's the life in your years. – **Abraham Lincoln**

"When you feel like giving up, remember why you held on for so long in the first place." - **Unknown**

"Life is short, live it. Love is rare, grab it. Anger is bad, dump it. Fear is awful, face it. Memories are sweet, cherish it." – **Unknown**

"Character cannot be developed in ease and quiet. Only through experience of trial and suffering can the soul be strengthened, ambition inspired, and success achieved."- **Helen Keller**

Rock bottom is good solid ground, and a dead end street is just a place to turn around. -**Buddy Buie and J.R. Cobb**

Encouraging Quotes

Do you give as much energy to your dreams as you do to your fears?
Unknown

Life is short, fragile and does not wait for anyone. There will NEVER be a perfect time to pursue your dreams & goals.
Unknown

Don't say you don't have enough time. You have exactly the same number of hours per day that were given to Helen Keller, Bill Gates, Michelangelo, Mother Teresa, Leonardo da Vinci, Thomas Jefferson, and Albert Einstein. **Unknown**

Even the greatest was once a beginner. Don't be afraid to take that first step. **Unknown**

"The first to apologize is the bravest. The first to forgive is the strongest. The first to forget is the happiest."
Unknown

"Never get tired of doing little things for your spouse. Sometimes those little things occupy the biggest part of their heart." **Unknown**

"There is nothing more admirable than two people who see eye-to-eye keeping house as man and wife, confounding their enemies, and delighting their friends." **Homer**

Encouraging Quotes

"When I am with you, the only place I want to be is closer."
Unknown

"Marriage succeeds only as lifetime commitment with no escape clauses." **Dr. James Dobson**

"A wise physician once said, 'The best medicine for humans is love.' Someone asked, 'What if it doesn't work?' He smiled and answered, 'Increase the dose'." **Unknown**

"I want a marriage more beautiful than my wedding."
Unknown

"Marriage is like a fine wine, if tended properly, it just gets better with age." **Unknown**

"Don't marry the person you think you can live with; marry only the individual you think you can't live without."-James C. Dobson

"Love is just a word until someone comes along and gives it meaning." **Unknown**

"Lean on each other's strengths. Forgive each other's weaknesses."
Unknown

Encouraging Scripture

Matthew 11:28-30
"Come to Me, all who are weary and heavy-laden, and I will give you rest. Take My yoke upon you and learn from Me, for I am gentle and humble in heart, and you will find rest for your souls. For My yoke is easy and My burden is light."

Romans 8:28
And we know that God causes all things to work together for good to those who love God, to those who are called according to His purpose.

Ephesians 5:25
Husbands, love your wives, just as Christ also loved the church and gave Himself up for her,

1 Peter 5:7
Casting all your anxiety on Him, because He cares for you.

1 Thessalonians 5:9-11
For God has not destined us for wrath, but for obtaining salvation through our Lord Jesus Christ, who died for us, so that whether we are awake or asleep, we will live together with Him. Therefore encourage one another and build up one another, just as you also are doing.

Encouraging Scripture

2 Corinthians 4:16-18
Therefore we do not lose heart, but though our outer man is decaying, yet our inner man is being renewed day by day. For momentary, light affliction is producing for us an eternal weight of glory far beyond all comparison, while we look not at the things which are seen, but at the things which are not seen; for the things which are seen are temporal, but the things which are not seen are eternal.

2 Thessalonians 2:16-17
Now may our Lord Jesus Christ Himself and God our Father, who has loved us and given us eternal comfort and good hope by grace, comfort and strengthen your hearts in every good work and word.

2 Thessalonians 3:16
Now may the Lord of peace Himself continually grant you peace in every] circumstance. The Lord be with you all!

2 Timothy 1:7
For God has not given us a spirit of timidity, but of power and love and discipline.

Colossians 3:15
Let the peace of Christ rule in your hearts, to which indeed you were called in one body; and be thankful.

Encouraging Scripture

Deuteronomy 31:6
Be strong and courageous, do not be afraid or tremble at them, for the Lord your God is the one who goes with you. He will not fail you or forsake you."

Ephesians 4:2-3
with all humility and gentleness, with patience, showing tolerance for one another in love, being diligent to preserve the unity of the Spirit in the bond of peace.

Galatians 6:9
Let us not lose heart in doing good, for in due time we will reap if we do not grow weary.

Hebrews 10:25
not forsaking our own assembling together, as is the habit of some, but encouraging one another; and all the more as you see the day drawing near.
Hebrews 13:8
Jesus Christ is the same yesterday and today and forever.

Hebrews 6:18
 so that by two unchangeable things in which it is impossible for God to lie, we who have taken refuge would have strong encouragement to take hold of the hope set before us.

Encouraging Scripture

Isaiah 40:31
Yet those who wait for the Lord
Will gain new strength;
They will mount up with wings like eagles,
They will run and not get tired,
They will walk and not become weary.

Isaiah 41:10
'Do not fear, for I am with you;
Do not anxiously look about you, for I am your God.
I will strengthen you, surely I will help you,
Surely I will uphold you with My righteous right hand.'

Isaiah 41:13
"For I am the Lord your God, who upholds your right hand,
Who says to you, 'Do not fear, I will help you.'

James 1:2-4
Consider it all joy, my brethren, when you encounter various
trials, knowing that the testing of your faith produces
endurance. And let endurance have its perfect result, so that
you may be perfect and complete, lacking in nothing.

John 14:27
Peace I leave with you; My peace I give to you; not as the
world gives do I give to you. Do not let your heart be
troubled, nor let it be fearful.

Encouraging Scripture

Jeremiah 29:11-14
For I know the plans that I have for you,' declares the Lord, 'plans for welfare and not for calamity to give you a future and a hope. Then you will call upon Me and come and pray to Me, and I will listen to you. You will seek Me and find Me when you search for Me with all your heart. I will be found by you,' declares the Lord, 'and I will restore your fortunes and will gather you from all the nations and from all the places where I have driven you,' declares the Lord, 'and I will bring you back to the place from where I sent you into exile.'

John 14:1-3
"Do not let your heart be troubled; believe in God, believe also in Me. In My Father's house are many dwelling places; if it were not so, I would have told you; for I go to prepare a place for you. If I go and prepare a place for you, I will come again and receive you to Myself, that where I am, there you may be also.

John 16:33
These things I have spoken to you, so that in Me you may have peace. In the world you have tribulation, but take courage; I have overcome the world."

Joshua 1:9
Have I not commanded you? Be strong and courageous! Do not tremble or be dismayed, for the Lord your God is with you wherever you go."

Encouraging Scripture

Mark 11:24
Therefore I say to you, all things for which you pray and ask, believe that you have received them, and they will be granted you.

1 Peter 4:8
Above all, keep fervent in your love for one another, because love covers a multitude of sins.

Philippians 4:13
I can do all things through Him who strengthens me.

Philippians 4:6-7
Be anxious for nothing, but in everything by prayer and supplication with thanksgiving let your requests be made known to God. And the peace of God, which surpasses all comprehension, will guard your hearts and your minds in Christ Jesus.

Romans 8:31
What then shall we say to these things? If God is for us, who is against us?

Proverbs 17:17
A friend loves at all times,
And a brother is born for adversity.

Encouraging Scripture

Proverbs 18:10
The name of the Lord is a strong tower;
The righteous runs into it and is safe.

Proverbs 3:5-6
Trust in the Lord with all your heart
And do not lean on your own understanding.
In all your ways acknowledge Him,
And He will make your paths straight.

Proverbs 30:5
Every word of God is tested;
He is a shield to those who take refuge in Him.

Psalm 118:14
The Lord is my strength and song,
And He has become my salvation.

Psalm 119:50
This is my comfort in my affliction,
That Your word has revived me.

Psalm 34:8
 O taste and see that the Lord is good;
How blessed is the man who takes refuge in Him!

Encouraging Scripture

Psalm 16:5-8
The Lord is the portion of my inheritance and my cup;
You support my lot.
 The lines have fallen to me in pleasant places;
Indeed, my heritage is beautiful to me.
 I will bless the Lord who has counseled me;
Indeed, my mind instructs me in the night.
 I have set the Lord continually before me;
Because He is at my right hand, I will not be shaken.

Psalm 18:32-36
The God who girds me with strength
And makes my way blameless?
He makes my feet like hinds' feet,
And sets me upon my high places.
He trains my hands for battle,
So that my arms can bend a bow of bronze.
You have also given me the shield of Your salvation,
And Your right hand upholds me;
And Your gentleness makes me great.
You enlarge my steps under me,
And my feet have not slipped.

Psalm 27:14
Wait for the Lord;
Be strong and let your heart take courage;
Yes, wait for the Lord.

Encouraging Scripture

Psalm 27:1
The Lord is my light and my salvation;
Whom shall I fear?
The Lord is the defense of my life;
Whom shall I dread?

Psalm 46:1-3
God is our refuge and strength,
A very present help in trouble.
 Therefore we will not fear, though the earth should change
And though the mountains slip into the heart of the sea;
 Though its waters roar and foam,
Though the mountains quake at its swelling pride. Selah.

Psalm 55:22
Cast your burden upon the Lord and He will sustain you;
He will never allow the righteous to be shaken.

Psalm 28:7
The Lord is my strength and my shield;
My heart trusts in Him, and I am helped;
Therefore my heart exults,
And with my song I shall thank Him.

Psalm 37:4
Delight yourself in the Lord;
And He will give you the desires of your heart.

Encouraging Scripture

Psalm 121:1-8
I will lift up my eyes to the mountains;
From where shall my help come?
My help comes from the Lord,
Who made heaven and earth.
He will not allow your foot to slip;
He who keeps you will not slumber.
Behold, He who keeps Israel
Will neither slumber nor sleep.
The Lord is your keeper;
The Lord is your shade on your right hand.
The sun will not smite you by day,
Nor the moon by night.
The Lord will protect you from all evil;
He will keep your soul.
The Lord will guard your going out and your coming in
From this time forth and forever.

Psalm 31:24
Be strong and let your heart take courage,
All you who hope in the Lord.

Romans 15:4-5
For whatever was written in earlier times was written for our
instruction, so that through perseverance and the
encouragement of the Scriptures we might have hope. Now
may the God who gives perseverance and encouragement
grant you to be of the same mind with one another according
to Christ Jesus,

Encouraging Scripture

Psalm 34:4
I sought the Lord, and He answered me,
And delivered me from all my fears.

Romans 5:1
Therefore, having been justified by faith, we have peace with
God through our Lord Jesus Christ,

Psalm 55:22
Cast your burden upon the Lord and He will sustain you;
He will never allow the righteous to be shaken.

Romans 15:13
Now may the God of hope fill you with all joy and peace in
believing, so that you will abound in hope by the power of the
Holy Spirit.

Romans 8:38-39
For I am convinced that neither death, nor life, nor angels, nor
principalities, nor things present, nor things to come, nor
powers, nor height, nor depth, nor any other created thing,
will be able to separate us from the love of God, which is in
Christ Jesus our Lord.

Final Thoughts

It is my hope and desire that you have found this book useful in your quest to encourage your Bride. Now you have the opportunity to put your knowledge into action. It is not enough to know what to do, you must do it!!

Make the investment of your Time, Talents and Treasures and you will see the most incredible return in your relationship with your Bride. She deserves a great man and you have the opportunity to be that great man for her.

Remember, you can never ever tell her "I LOVE YOU" to much and you can never ever tell her "YOU ARE BEAUTIFUL" to much. You need to have those phrases tattooed on you your heart and mind and strive to make them an integral part of your daily routine.

If you do these things to encourage your Bride and you are a father, you will also be showing you sons how to treat their future Bride and helping set the expectations for your daughter's future husband.

Blessings to you and your family!

Paul Beersdorf

Suggested Books to Read

If you were only going to read one book (other than this one of course), read the first one at the top of the list. I have read it and re-read it many times! **If Only He Knew** is a powerful book that will help you better understand your Bride.

If Only He Knew   - Gary Smalley

The 5 Love Languages   - Gary Chapman

Father's & Daughter's   - Jack & Jerry Schreur

The Language of Love   - Gary Smalley &

                                                             John Trent

"Daddy's Home"   - Greg Johnson &

                                                             Mike Yorkey

Hidden Keys of a Loving Lasting Marriage - Gary Smalley

The Hidden Value of a Man   - Gary Smalley &

                                                             John Trent

What Kids Need Most in a Dad   - Tim Hansel

Suggested Books

Father's & Son's	- Jack & Jerry Schreur
Point Man	- Steve Farrar
Go the Distance	- John Trent
In the Grip of Grace	- Max Lucado
Love for a Lifetime	- Dr. James Dobson
Staying in Love for a Lifetime	- Ed Wheat M.D.
Dare to Discipline	- Dr. James Dobson
The New Dare to Discipline	- Dr. James Dobson
Straight Talk	- Dr. James Dobson
Beside Every Great Dad	- Swihart & Canfield
The Road Unseen	- Jerry Jenkins
Daddy's Home	- Steve Schnur
The Power of the Promise Kept	- Many
7 Promises of a Promise Keeper	- Many
Hedges	- Jerry Jenkins
Rookie Dad	- Rick Epstein
She Calls me Daddy	- Wolgemuth

Suggested Books

Disciplines in Grace	- Hughes
Locking Arms	- Weber
4 Pillars of a Man	- Weber
Intended for Pleasure	- Ed Wheat M.D.
Life on the Edge	- Dr. James Dobson
Standing Tall	- Farrar
As Iron Sharpens Iron	- Howard & William Hendricks
Tender Warrior	- Weber
The 5 Habits of Smart Dads	- Lewis
Raising a Modern Day Knight	- Lewis
Outdoor Insights	- Steve Chapman
What a Difference a Daddy Makes	- Lehman
Who's in Charge Here	- Barnes
I Love You, But Why are We so Different?	- Layhaye

Suggested Books

Dating Your Mate	- Bundschuh & Gilbert
Twice Pardoned	- Morris
The Strong Willed Child	- Dr. James Dobson
Putting Amazing Back into Grace	- Horton
The Nature of Spiritual Growth	- Wesley
How a Many Stands up for Christ	- Gilbert
In Search of Excellence	- Peters et.al.
A Passion for Excellence	- Peters et.al.
7 Habits of Highly Effective People	- Covey
Love is a Decision	- Smalley & Trent
The Power of Personal Integrity	-Charles Dyer
Flowers on Tuesday	- Paul Beersdorf

Other Resources

Below are some additional websites and resources you might want to consider and might prove helpful as you start to encourage your Bride.

I do not endorse any of these sites this is just a list for your convenience.

E-Greeting Cards - a great way to encourage your Bride

www.bluemountain.com
www.123greetings.com
www.americangreetings.com
www.smilebox.com

Marriage Retreats

www.winshape.org/Retreat/2.0/

Ideas for Dates and Places

www.tripadvisor.com
www.urbanspoon.com
www.yelp.com

Name a Star after your Bride

www.starregistry.com
www.nameastarlive.com

Several Apps for Dedicating a Song to Your Bride

Songnote (iOS; free)
MTV Dedicate (iOS; free)
ShoutOut Radio (iOS; free)
Songdedicate (iOS; free)
Songed (web; free)

Singing Telegram

www.gigmasters.com/services/Singing-Telegram
www.americansingingtelegrams.com

Help with Poem Writing

www.aipoem.com
www.poemofquotes.com
www.rhymer.com

Great Romantic/Chick Flick Movies to Rent or Buy.

- While You Were Sleeping
- Sleepless in Seattle
- Mama Mia
- Pride & Prejudice
- Emma
- My Big Fat Greek Wedding
- Romeo & Juliet
- Sound of Music
- 7 Brides for 7 Brothers
- Beauty and the Beast
- The Bachelor
- Little Women
- Anne of Green Gables
- Kate & Leopold
- Only You
- Runaway Bride
- 27 Dresses
- Bride Wars
- Made of Honor
- The Prince and Me
- The Princess Bride
- 13 Going on 30
- The Ultimate Gift
- Maid in Manhattan
- Guess Who
- P.S. I love You
- Sense and Sensibility
- An Affair to Remember
- You've Got Mail
- The Wedding Planner
- My Best Friend's Wedding
- Father of the Bride

Great Romantic/Chick Flick Movies to Rent or Buy.

- Father of the Bride 2
- Hitch
- How to Lose a Guy in 10 Days
- Moms Night Out
- Failure to Launch
- Legally Blonde
- Legally Blond 2
- Breakfast at Tiffany's
- Princess Diaries
- The Proposal
- The Devil Wears Prada
- Miss Congeniality
- Sweet Home Alabama
- Steel Magnolias
- The Notebook
- What Women Want
- Just Like Heaven
- Sydney White
- A Walk to Remember
- Gone With The Wind
- Something's Got to Give
- The Cinderella Story
- Titanic
- Raising Helen
- Ghost
- Terms of Endearment
- Fried Green Tomatoes
- Serendipity
- Can't Buy Me Love
- First Knight
- Forget Paris
- Phantom of the Opera

Romantic Songs to Download

I started to recommend some songs, but then realized just how old I was by the choices that came to mind. Therefore, my best suggestion is to refer you to several websites that have listings of the top love/romantic songs and let you pick some out for yourself.

They key is that you find some songs that can be just for you and your Bride.

billboard.com/articles/list/1538839/top-50-love-songs-of-all-time

top40.about.com/od/top10lists/tp/top100lovesongs.htm

mag.weddingcentral.com.au/music/songs/love-songs.htm

tasteofcountry.com/top-100-country-love-songs/

listology.com/list/100-greatest-rb-love-songs

play.google.com/store?hl=en

apple.com/itunes/

Suggested Weekly Schedule for Basic Encouragement

For those of you who do not know where to start and need an outline of what to do, below is a suggested weekly calendar for encouraging your Bride. Remember, this is meant to be **very basic** and as your grow and mature, you should move beyond these basic ideas and timelines.

Monday -Friday-

- Kiss her goodbye and tell her you love her

- Text message in the morning to encourage her

- Text message in the afternoon to encourage her

- At some point in the day, remind her how beautiful she is and how lucky you are to be married to her

- Give her a kiss and hug when you get home (comment positively on how she looks)

- Tell her about your day and then ask her about her day and focus on her as she talks

- Ask if there are any chores or "to do's

- Kiss her good night and give her a big hug

Saturday

- If you are out running errands- send her an encouraging text message

- Continue with Kiss and hug to wake up and kiss and hug when you go to bed

- Date night - have something fun planned

- Tell her how beautiful she is

- Tell her you love her multiple time today

Sunday

- Continue with Kiss and hug to wake up and kiss and hug when you go to bed

- Tell her how beautiful she is

- Attend church and worship God together

- Take a nap together

- Fix her supper tonight and let her relax

  - Tell her you love her multiple times today

I hope you enjoyed the book and it proves helpful in drawing you closer to your Bride and encouraging her on a regular basis.

If you would like to provide any feedback, comments or thoughts, you can reach me at:

paulbeersdorf@gmail.com

The End

www.ingramcontent.com/pod-product-compliance
Lightning Source LLC
Chambersburg PA
CBHW071620040426
42452CB00009B/1414